Piano *light*

Spirituals & Gospels

24 leichte Arrangements

ED 9557

SCHOTT

Mainz · London · Madrid · New York · Paris · Tokyo · Toronto

Inhalt / Contents

Bestell-Nr. / Order No. ED 9557

ISMN M-001-13380-7

© 2002 Schott Musik International, Mainz
Editor: Harald Wingerter
The Harlem Gospel Singers – eine Produktion der BB Promotion GmbH
Cover Photo: Nacho Arías

Printed in Germany · BSS 50 952

www.schott-music.com

Amazing Grace

Traditional
Arr.: H. Luedeman

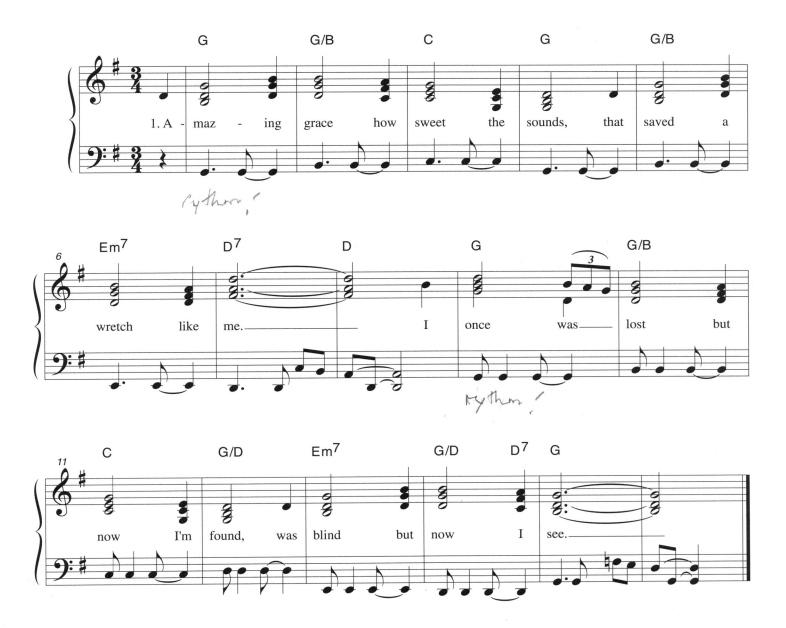

2. 'T was grace that taught my heart to fear,
And grace my fears relieved.
How precious did that grace appear,
The hour I first believed.

3. When we've been there ten thousand years,
Bright shining as the sun.
We've no less days to sing God's praise,
Than when we first begun.

4. Through many dangers, toils and snares,
I have already come.
This grace hath brought me safe thus far,
And grace will lead me home.

4

Amen

Traditional
Arr.: H. Luedeman

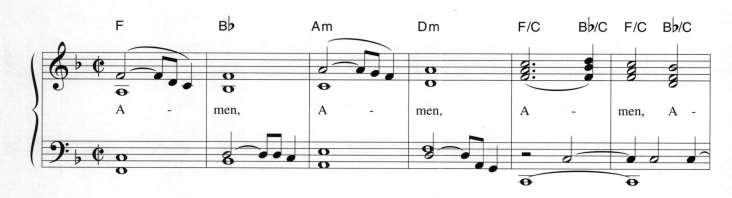

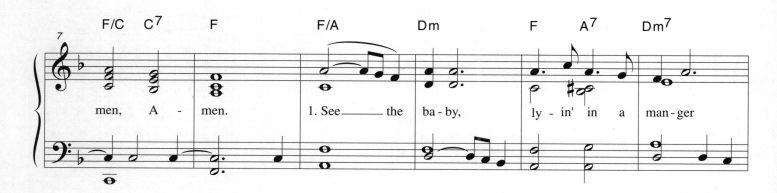

2. Amen, …
See him in the temple, talking to the Elders,
How they marveled at his wisdom.

3. Amen, …
See him in the garden, praying to his father
In deepest sorrow.

4. Amen, …
Yes, he is my savior, Jesus did to help us,
And he rose on Easter.

5. Amen, …
Hallelujah in the kingdom with my savior,
Amen, Amen.

Deep River

Traditional
Arr.: H. Luedeman

Dry Bones

Traditional
Arr.: H. Luedeman

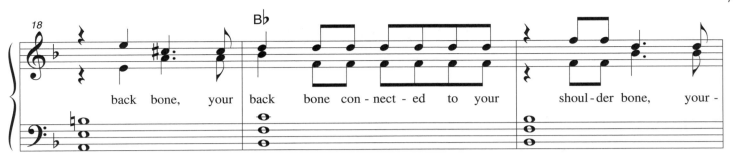

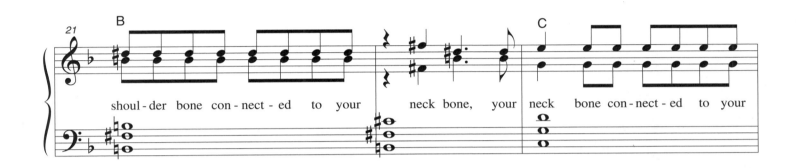

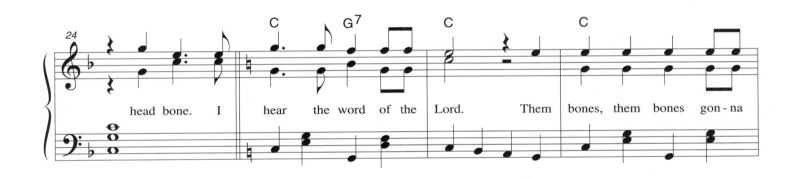

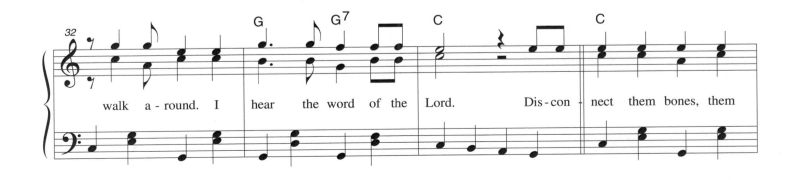

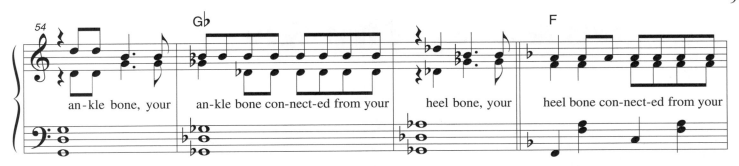

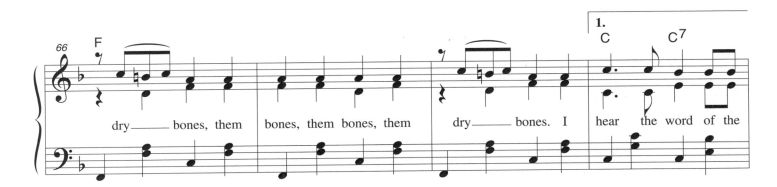

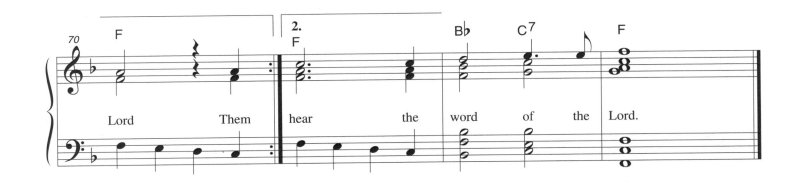

Down By The Riverside

Traditional
Arr.: H. Luedeman

Gimme That Old Time Religion

Traditional
Arr.: H. Luedeman

Glory, Hallelujah!
(John Brown's Body)

Traditional
Arr.: H. Luedeman

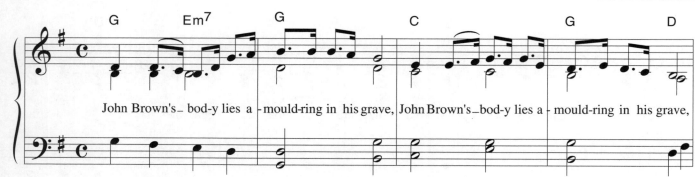

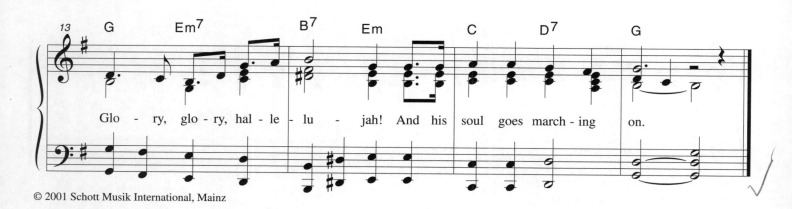

Go Down, Moses

Traditional
Arr.: H. Luedeman

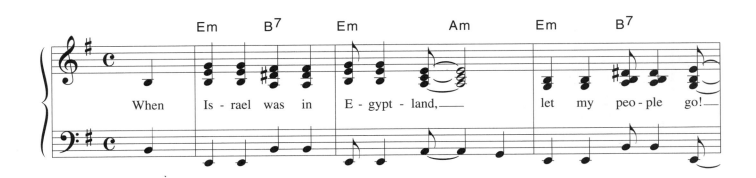

When Is - rael was in E - gypt - land,____ let my peo - ple go!

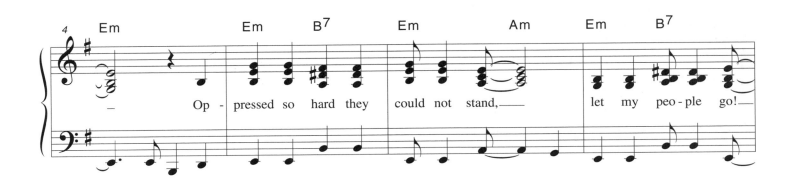

Op - pressed so hard they could not stand,____ let my peo - ple go!

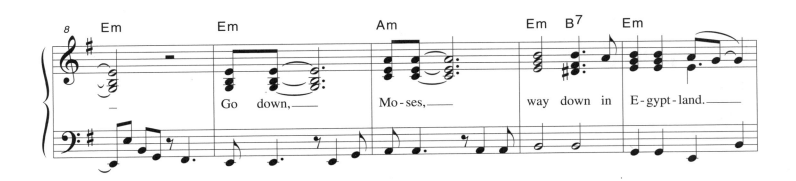

Go down,____ Mo - ses,____ way down in E - gypt - land.____

Tell Pha to let my - peo - ple go.____

Go, Tell It On The Mountains

Traditional
Arr.: H. Luedeman

Good News!
The Chariot's Comin'

Traditional
Arr.: H. Luedeman

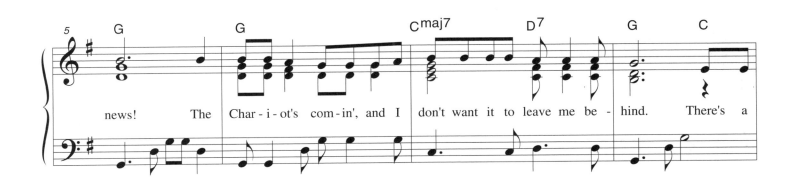

Heaven

Traditional
Arr.: H. Luedeman

I got shoes, ___ you got shoes, ___ all God's chil-dren got

shoes, my Lord. ___ When I get to heav-en, gon-na put on them shoes, ___ I'm gon-na

walk, yeah, ___ walk, yeah, ___ I'm gon-na walk all o-ver God's heav-en, yeah, ___ Lord,

heav-en, yeah, ___ Lord, heav-en, Lord! ___ Ev'-ry-bo-dy's talk-in' of but

2.
I got a robe, you got a robe,
All God's children got robes, my Lord.
When I get to heaven gonna wear that robe,
I'm gonna shout, yeah, shout, yeah,
I'm gonna shout all over God's heaven, yeah, Lord,
heaven, yeah, Lord, heaven, Lord!
Ev'rybody's talkin' of but no one's ever goin' to heaven,
yeah, Lord, heaven, Lord!
I'm gonna shout all over God's heaven, oh, yeah!

3.
 I got wings, you got wings,
All God's children got wings, my Lord.
When I get to heaven gonna use them wings,
I'm gonna fly, yeah, fly, yeah,
I'm gonna fly all over God's heaven, yeah, Lord,
heaven, yeah, Lord, heaven, Lord!
Ev'rybody's talkin' of but no one's ever goin' to heaven,
yeah, Lord, heaven, Lord!
I'm gonna fly all over God's heaven, oh, yeah!

18

He's Got The Whole World In His Hands

Traditional
Arr.: H. Luedeman

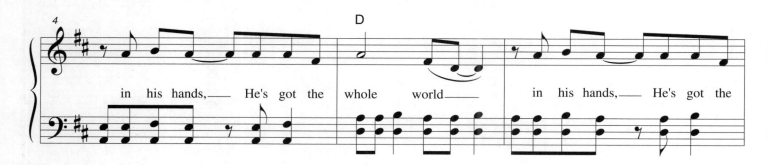

© 2001 Schott Musik International, Mainz

Joshua Fit The Battle Of Jericho

Traditional
Arr.: H. Luedeman

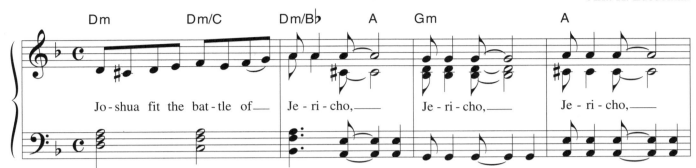

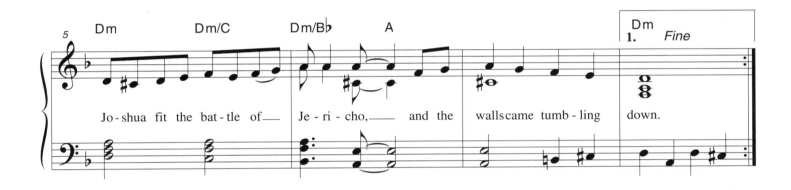

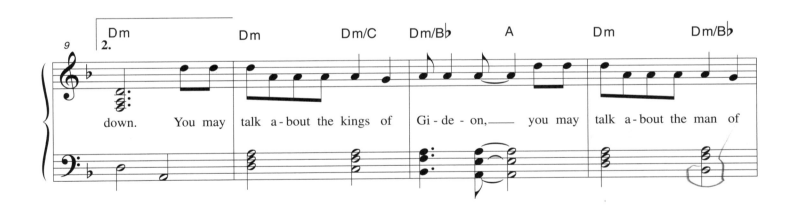

Kum ba yah

Traditional
Arr.: H. Luedeman

Michael, Row The Boat Ashore

Traditional
Arr.: H. Luedeman

Nobody Knows
The Trouble I've Seen

Traditional
Arr.: H. Luedeman

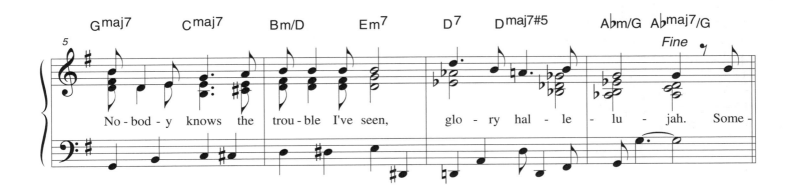

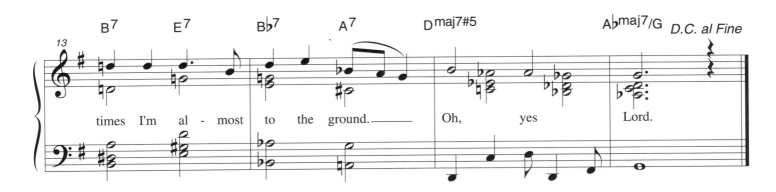

Oh Happy Day

Traditional
Arr.: H. Luedeman

Oh hap-py day, oh hap-py day_____ when Je - sus

washed,_____ oh when he washed,_____ when Je - sus washed,_____

he washed my sin a - way. Oh hap-py day, oh hap-py

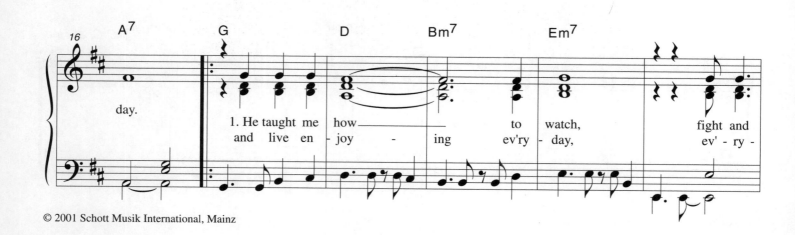

day.
1. He taught me how_____ to watch, fight and
and live en - joy - ing ev'ry - day, ev'ry -

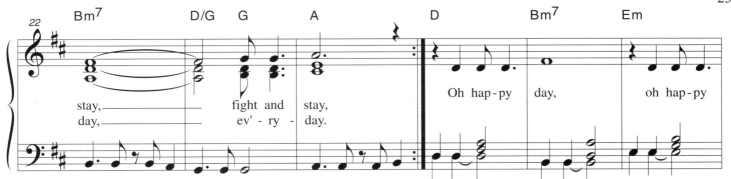

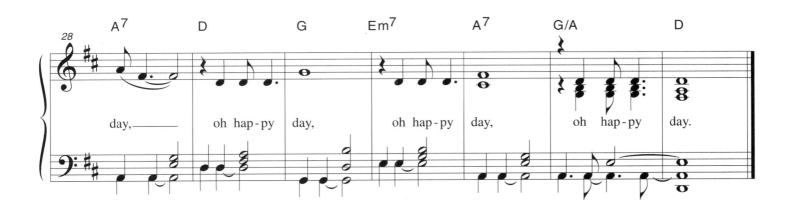

Rev. Charles Lyles (p) &
The Harlem Gospel Singers

Photo: Olivier Michel

Oh, When The Saints

Traditional
Arr.: H. Luedeman

Oh, when the saints go march-in' in, oh, when the

saints go march - in' in, I want to be in that

num - ber, oh, when the saints go march - in' in.

2.
And when the stars begin to shine,
And when the stars begin to shine,
I want to be in that number,
Oh, when the stars begin to shine.

3.
When Gabriel blows in his horn,
When Gabriel blows in his horn,
I want to be in that number,
When Gabriel blows in his horn.

4.
And when the band begins to play,
And when the band begins to play,
I want to be in that number,
Oh, when the band begins to play.

5.
And when they crown him King of Kings,
And when they crown him King of Kings,
I want to be in that number,
Oh, when they crown him King of Kings.

Rock My Soul

Traditional
Arr.: H. Luedeman

Over In The Gloryland

Traditional
Arr.: H. Luedeman

Sometimes I Feel
Like A Motherless Child

Traditional
Arr.: H. Luedeman

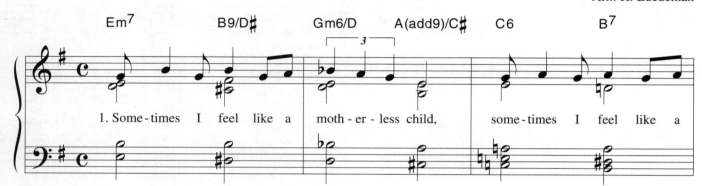

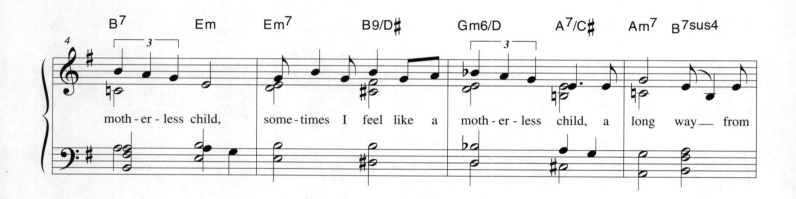

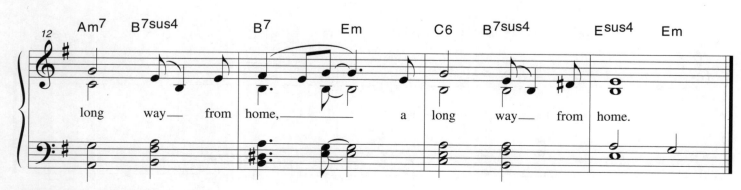

Steal Away

Traditional
Arr.: H. Luedeman

1. Steal a - way, steal a - way, steal a - way to Je - sus. Steal a - way,

steal a - way home. I ain't got long to stay here. My Lord calls me, He calls me by the

thun - der; the trum - pet sounds with - in my soul! I ain't got long to stay here.

2.
Steal away, steal away,
steal away to Jesus.
Steal away, steal away home.
I ain't got long to stay here.
Green trees a-bending,
Poor sinner stands a-trembling;
The trumpet sounds within my soul!
I ain't got long to stay here.

Swing Low, Sweet Chariot

Traditional
Arr.: H. Luedeman

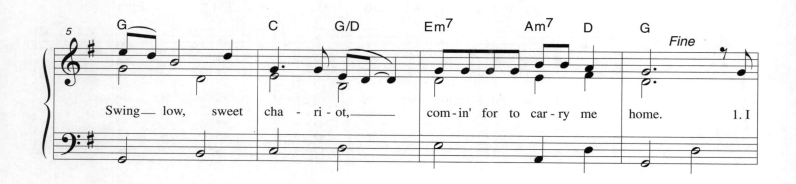

Wade In The Water

Traditional
Arr.: H. Luedeman

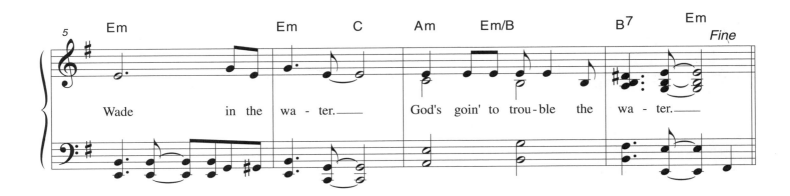

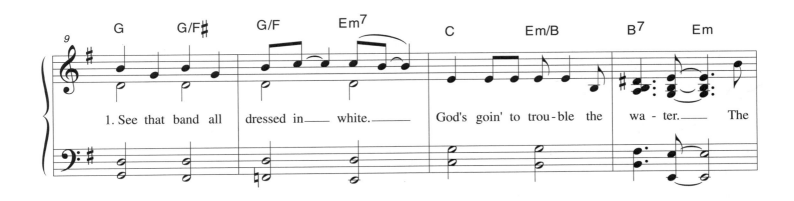

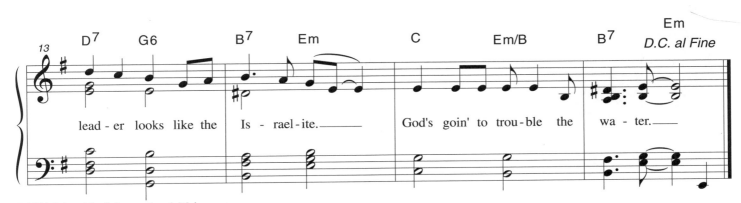

plus CD

Gabriel Bock

Playing **Latin PIANO**

A new way to learn the Samba and Bossa Nova

Die neue EINMALIGE Methode ❧ die Finger tanzen Samba und Bossa

Including:
One Note Samba
Manha de Carneval
Samba de Orfeu
Summer Samba

ED 9262

SCHOTT

MA 106